FACTS AT YOUR FINGERTIPS

EXPLORERS

DAVID MARSHALL

SIMON & SCHUSTER
YOUNG BOOKS

Commissioning editor: Daphne Butler
Design and artwork: SPL Design
Photographs: ZEFA, except for
Hutchinson (20)
Science Photo Library (29)
Typesetting and layout: Quark Xpress

First published in Great Britain in 1992
by Simon & Schuster Young Books

Simon & Schuster Young Books
Campus 400, Maylands Avenue
Hemel Hempstead, Herts HP2 7EZ

© 1992 Simon & Schuster Young Books

Printed and bound in Belgium
by Proost International Book Production

A catalogue record for this book
is available from the British Library
ISBN 0 7500 1083 5

CONTENTS

EARLY

EXPLORERS

Early explorers often travelled in search of food, or new places to settle when their tribes became too big. They only went where it was easy to travel, and the land was welcoming and similar to the home they had left. ►

◄ Most people thought the Earth was flat and that travelling too far would mean falling off the edge. It took a very special sort of person to brave unknown mountains, oceans and deserts.

Some explorers were searching for fame—others for riches or to spread their religion. Some were just curious. Whatever their reasons for travelling all explorers share a desire for knowledge and have great courage. ►

EGYPTIANS, GREEKS AND ROMANS

About 1500 BC, the Egyptians crossed the desert and sailed down Africa's east coast to a place called Punt. They were looking for myrrh which they used to embalm their dead. Later, Greek traders travelled out into the Atlantic Ocean searching for new people to trade with. Later still, the Romans took their civilisation and ways with them as they built up their huge empire.

An ancient village at Bants Carn on the Scilly Isles—as early as 1000 BC traders may have come here searching for tin. ▼

About 330 BC, Pytheas, a Greek explorer, sailed past the British Isles and on northward until ice blocked his way. He visited a land he called "Ultima Thule". Today, we think he reached Norway or Iceland.

VIKINGS

Possible routes taken by Vikings Bjarni Herjolfsson and Leif Ericsson, probably the first Europeans to visit North America.

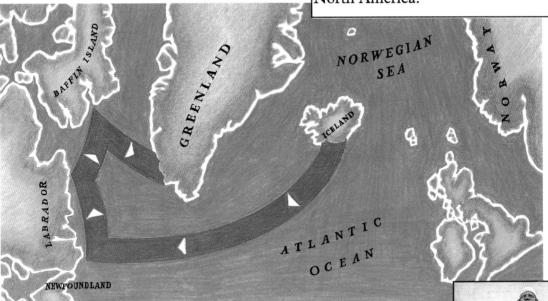

BAFFIN ISLAND

GREENLAND

NORWEGIAN SEA

NORWAY

ICELAND

LABRADOR

ATLANTIC OCEAN

NEWFOUNDLAND

Around AD 800, Vikings began to search for new lands because their population had grown too great for their homelands. They spread to Britain, France and Iceland. In 982, Erik the Red was banished from Norway to Iceland as a punishment. He explored to the west of Iceland and discovered Greenland. Later, Bjarni Herjolfsson was blown off course and probably landed in Canada. In AD 1000, Erik's son, Leif Ericsson, sailed from Iceland to explore this new land in the west.

Statue of Leif Ericsson in Reykjavik, Iceland. ➤

Coastline of Iceland much as Leif Ericsson might have seen it. ▼

MARCO POLO

In 1271, Marco Polo left Venice to travel to the court of Kublai Khan, emperor of the Mongols. His court was in Khanbalik, today's Beijing, the capital city of China. Marco journeyed overland for 4 years by way of Jerusalem, Baghdad and the Old Silk Road. He stayed in China for 17 years, travelling around as a court official, before returning to Venice by way of Malaysia, Malabar on the Indian coast, Ceylon (now Sri Lanka) and the Persian Gulf.

▲ Venice was a great trading centre when Marco Polo was born there in 1254. He left with his uncles to travel to China when he was just 17 years old. He returned to his homeland 24 years later, telling wondrous tales of life in the East which few people, at that time, could believe.

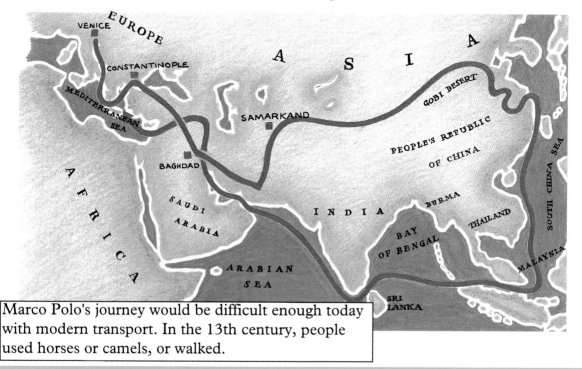

Marco Polo's journey would be difficult enough today with modern transport. In the 13th century, people used horses or camels, or walked.

HENRY THE NAVIGATOR

Henry the Navigator, third son of John I of Portugal, sponsored and guided over 50 Portuguese voyages of exploration. In 1419, two of his explorers discovered Madeira and claimed it for Portugal. Over the next 40 years, others travelled further and further down the African coast. Henry started a school of navigation in Sagres where he collected together astronomers, mathematicians, mapmakers, boat-builders and sailors. They built a new kind of ship called a caravel. Without this, the voyages of discovery could never have happened.

The belief in navigation and careful exploration started by Henry, led to many important voyages of discovery in the 50 years after his death in 1460.

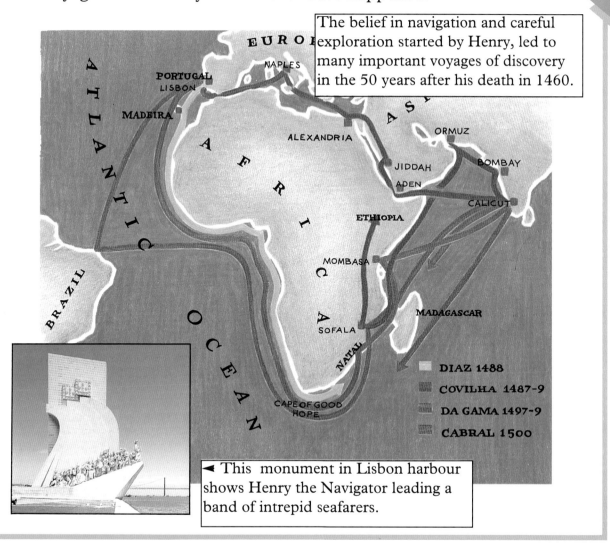

DIAZ 1488
COVILHA 1487-9
DA GAMA 1497-9
CABRAL 1500

◄ This monument in Lisbon harbour shows Henry the Navigator leading a band of intrepid seafarers.

EXPLORING OVER

THE OCEANS

The first ships were canoes with sails rather like the outrigger canoes still used by Pacific Islanders. It was not until the 12th century that ships started to have decks, and another century before they were ready to make long voyages. ➤

◄ Once out of sight of land people needed a means of finding their way—a means of navigation. The stars and the moon were an early choice but they're invisible during the day.

The first instrument invented for navigation was the magnetic compass but this only showed the direction of north. Sailors also needed to know how *far* north or west they were. Many instruments have been invented—today, we use radar and satellites as well.➤

CHRISTOPHER COLUMBUS

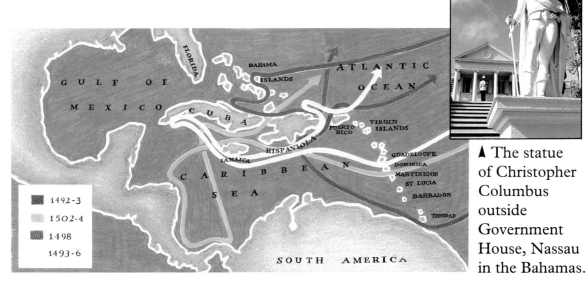

1492-3
1502-4
1498
1493-6

▲ The statue of Christopher Columbus outside Government House, Nassau in the Bahamas.

Christopher Columbus was born in Genoa, Italy, in 1451. From an early age all he wanted to do was to travel and explore. He believed he could reach India and China by sailing westward, and in 1492, he set off with three ships provided by the Spanish Court. Eventually, he landed on the Bahamas in the Caribbean and thought he had reached islands off India and China. He made three more voyages to the "West Indies", finding even more islands and also landed in South America in 1498—but he thought it was just another island.

Hispaniola (now the Dominican Republic in the Caribbean) as Columbus would have seen it in 1493. ▼

EARLY EXPLORERS OF AMERICA

Between 1499 and 1502 another Italian, Amerigo Vespucci, made three voyages to Columbus's "West Indies". Exploring the coast of Brazil, Amerigo realised that this was not an island off Asia, but a whole new continent. It was named America for all time.►

◄ In 1519, Hernán Cortés, a Spaniard, sailed from Cuba with 600 men, to the coast of what is now Mexico. Further inland, Aztec Indians ruled a wealthy civilisation of 20 million people. Cortés set out to overthrow them and seize their gold. By 1521, Moctezuma, the Aztec leader, was dead and Cortés was ruling on behalf of Spain. Twenty years later, only 6 million Aztecs remained.

Francisco Pizarro was another Spanish adventurer interested only in gold. In 1533, he found and looted Cuzco, the capital of the Inca nation. Cuzco is high in the Andes mountains and to reach it, the Spaniards marched long distances along precarious mountain ledges. Pizzaro conquered the Incas but was such a bad ruler his own men killed him in 1541. ►

AROUND THE WORLD

Ferdinand Magellan set out in 1519 with five ships to show that it was possible to reach the Moluccas by sailing westward. After a dreadful journey, two of the ships finally made it across the Pacific to the Philippines where Magellan was killed. The ships sailed on, found the Moluccas, and eventually the first one got back to Spain in 1522.

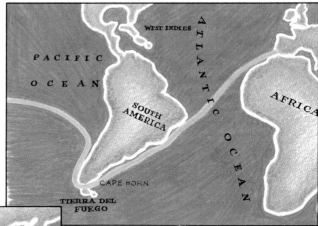

To reach the Pacific Ocean, Magellan sailed through a treacherous channel between the tip of South America and Tierra del Fuego. It is now called the Magellan Strait.▼

The Philippines much as they would have seemed to Magellan before he was killed in a local skirmish in 1521. ▼

THE SOUTHERN CONTINENT

People had long believed there should be a huge a southern continent the same kind of size as Asia—but no one had found it. Searching for this continent, Abel Tasman, a Dutchman, sailed into the vast Southern Ocean in 1642. Completely missing Australia, he discovered the island now named after him—Tasmania. He was then blown off course and found New Zealand. It was not until 1683, when William Dampier sailed along the north west coast of Australia and across to New Guinea that there was any real idea of the size and extent of Australia. Between 1769 and 1775, James Cook surveyed New Zealand, sailed up the east coast of Australia and round Antarctica twice.

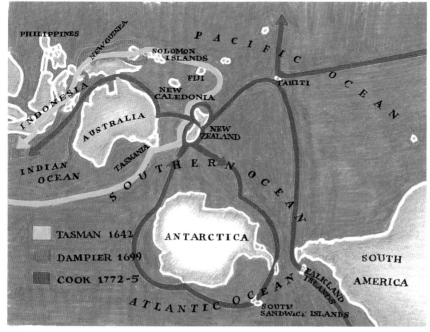

▲ Hobart—capital city of Tasmania. It was not until 1798, when Bass sailed through the strait between Tasmania and Australia that Tasmania was proved a separate island.

◄ By 1700, explorers had realised that a vast southern continent the size of Asia, did not exist.

CAPTAIN COOK

In 1768, Captain James Cook set out on his first voyage of discovery. With a group of scientists aboard, he sailed south from Tahiti then west on a course 40°S, until he came to the coast of New Zealand. After sailing round New Zealand, he headed on westward landing at Botany Bay in Australia. Calling it New South Wales, he claimed it for Britain. He turned north and sailed up the coast, nearly foundering on the Great Barrier Reef before sailing through the Torres Strait.

▲ A replica of *New Endeavour*—the ship used by James Cook on his first voyage of exploration in the Pacific.

◄ Cook spent six months on his first voyage charting the coasts of New Zealand. It was a masterly piece of work—the first time a survey had been carried out methodically, and it set high scientific standards for future explorers.

Cook's second voyage, in 1772, took him across the Antarctic Circle and round the world at previously unsailed latitudes. He charted many Pacific Islands and later crossed the Antarctic Circle a second time, discovering South Georgia and the South Sandwich Islands. This epic voyage lasted for three years and showed once and for all that the "Great Southern Continent" did not exist.

Tahiti—Cook's favourite starting point in the Pacific Ocean. ►

Kealakekua Bay, Hawaii, where Captain Cook was killed in 1780. ▼

Cook's final voyage started in 1776 and lasted until his death in 1780. His task was to find a route round the north of America from the Pacific side. Sailing due north from Tahiti, he discovered the Hawaiian Islands. He then headed east till he sighted the American coast and turning northward surveyed the coasts of Canada and Alaska. He decided there was no sea route round America when ice barred his way. After returning to the Hawaiian Islands, Cook was killed in a squabble over a stolen boat.

17

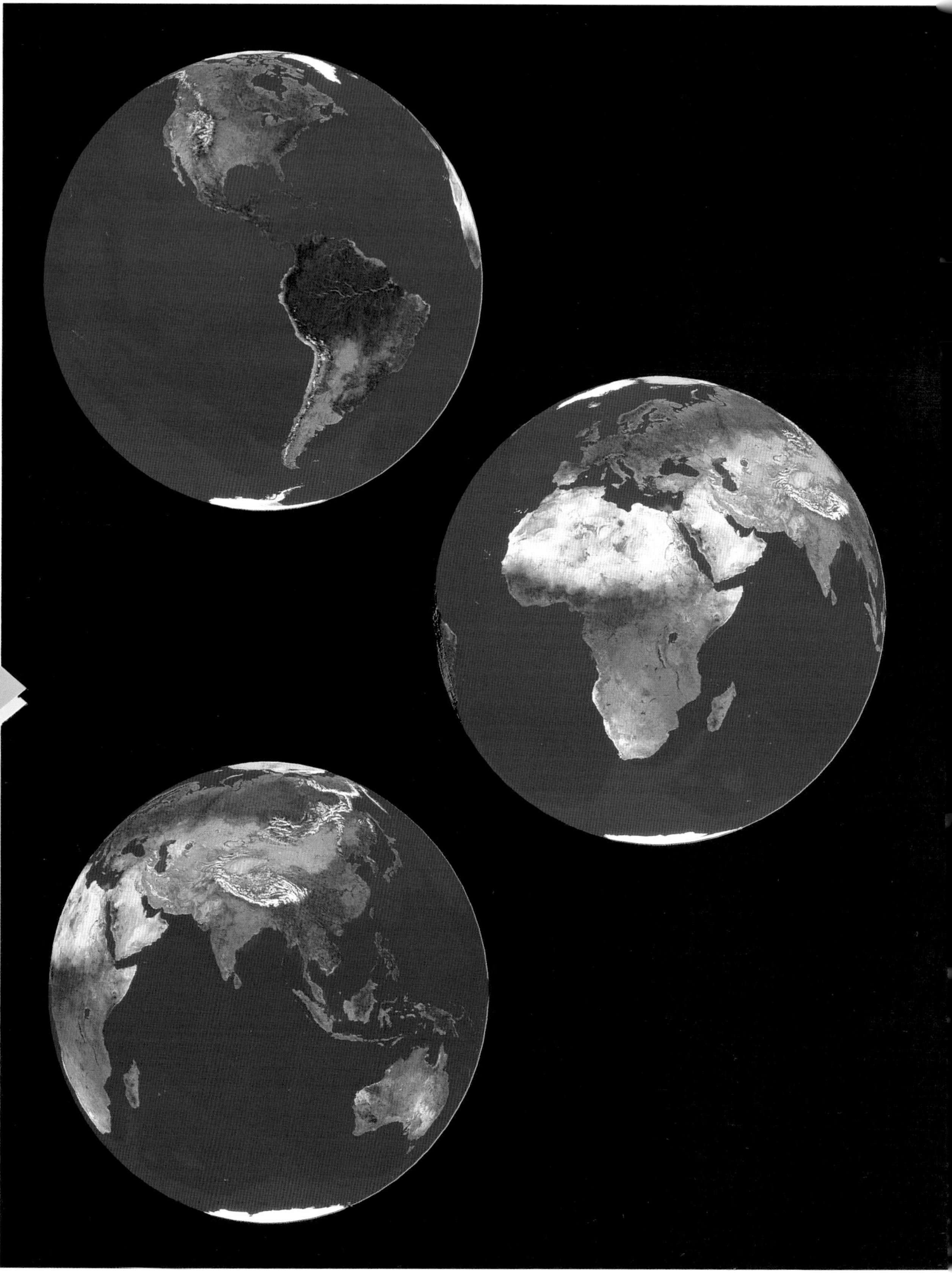

THE WORLD

DISCOVERED

There were many years of painstaking travel before most of the world was known. Many people perished crossing deserts, scaling mountains and following rivers, but explorers are stubborn people determined to reach their goal. ➤

◄ Although most of the Earth's land surface was explored and understood by the beginning of the 20th century, the seas and oceans were still a mystery. Even today, there are still secrets waiting to be discovered.

Perhaps the greatest challenge today, is the exploration of space. Being able to walk and breathe beyond our atmosphere would have been bewildering to early explorers—and even to people only 50 years ago. ➤

AFRICA

In 1795, Mungo Park was asked by the Africa Association to explore the course of the River Niger in west Africa. He set out from Gambia and eventually reached the River Niger at Ségou in modern Mali. He went about 120 kilometres downstream, before his supplies ran out and he had to return. He tried again in 1805, and finding a boat at Timbuktu, he sailed down the Niger but was drowned at the Bussa Rapids in Nigeria.

The River Niger at Koton Karifi in Nigeria. ➤

Richard Burton and John Hanning Speke set off in 1857, from Bagamoyo on the east coast of Africa, to search for the source of the River Nile. About 800 kilometres inland, they reached Tabora where Arab traders told of a great lake to the north. Speke immediately wanted to visit this, but Burton persuaded him to keep going westward and they found Lake Tanganyika which is known as Burton's "discovery". Later, Speke visited the other lake which he named Victoria, and declared was the source of the River Nile. Burton wouldn't agree and they parted on very bad terms.

◄ Lake Tanganyika from Zaïre.

David Livingstone was a missionary, and an important explorer because he made careful notes and maps of his journeys. In 1855, he discovered the Victoria Falls on the Zambezi River and returned three years later, to sail up the Zambezi from the sea—a disastrous expedition during which his wife died. By 1867, he was setting out again to look for the source of the Nile, but he completely disappeared. He was found by H M Stanley, tired and broken at Ujiji on Lake Tanganyika in 1871. His health improved and, with Stanley, he explored the northern shores of Lake Tanganyika. Livingstone became more and more obsessed with the source of the Nile. He died in 1873, on the shores of Lake Bangweulu, still searching.

▲ The spectacular Victoria Falls on the River Zambezi, discovered by Livingstone in 1855.

▼ Stanley's journey across Africa.

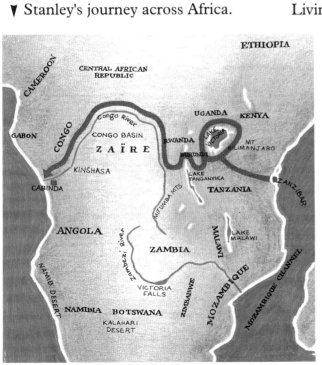

Stanley admired Livingstone and decided after his death to follow his ideas. He set off from Bogamoyo in 1874 with a well-equipped expedition. They went first to Lake Victoria proving that the only outlet was the Nile, and then on to Lake Tanganyika. Following the only river out of the lake he explored the length of the Congo/Zaire River. This has dangerous cataracts and flows thousands of kilometres through dense forest to the Atlantic Ocean. The journey took three years, turned Stanley's hair white, and killed two thirds of his expedition.

NORTH AMERICA

In July 1893, Alexander Mackenzie arrived at the Arctic Ocean having followed the great river flowing from the Great Slave Lake. He travelled through country like this in North West Territories, Canada. ▼

▲ Hudson Bay was discovered by Henry Hudson in 1610. However, after a mutiny on board his ship, Hudson, his son and seven companions were set adrift to die in the cold barren waste.

In 1804, Meriwether Lewis and William Clark led an expedition up the Missouri river from St Louis, across the Rocky Mountains, and down the Snake river to the Pacific Ocean. The Rocky Mountains were difficult to cross and a mighty barrier to exploration westward. ▼

▲ The city of Chicago at the south end of Lake Michigan. In 1680, when Robert La Salle came here, it was open country. La Salle travelled on south, and down the Mississippi to the Gulf of Mexico naming the whole area Louisiana and claiming it for France.

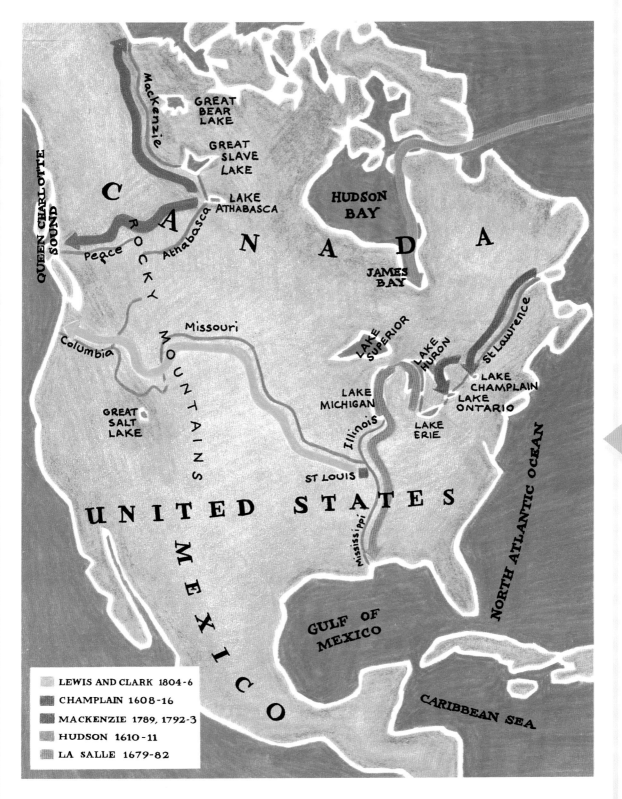

MACKENZIE
GREAT BEAR LAKE
GREAT SLAVE LAKE
LAKE ATHABASCA
Athabasca
C A N A D A
ROCKY
Peace
QUEEN CHARLOTTE SOUND
HUDSON BAY
JAMES BAY
St Lawrence
Missouri
LAKE SUPERIOR
LAKE HURON
Columbia
MOUNTAINS
LAKE CHAMPLAIN
LAKE ONTARIO
LAKE MICHIGAN
GREAT SALT LAKE
Illinois
LAKE ERIE
ST LOUIS
U N I T E D   S T A T E S
M E X I C O
Mississippi
NORTH ATLANTIC OCEAN
GULF OF MEXICO
CARIBBEAN SEA

23

LEWIS AND CLARK 1804-6
CHAMPLAIN 1608-16
MACKENZIE 1789, 1792-3
HUDSON 1610-11
LA SALLE 1679-82

AUSTRALIA

In 1860, an expedition led by Robert Burke and William Wills travelled from Victoria to the Gulf of Carpenteria in an attempt to cross the huge Australian continent. Only one man, King, survived the heat and lack of drinking water. ➤

TIMOR SEA

VAN DIEMEN GULF
ATTACK CREEK

GULF OF CARPENTARIA

STURT 1829-30, 1844-5

EYRE 1840-1

STUART 1860, 1861, 1862

BURKE AND WILLS 1860 1

MACDONNELL RANGES

SIMPSON DESERT

GREAT DIVIDING RANGE

LAKE EYRE

FLINDERS RANGES

BARRIER RANGE

LAKE TORRENS

MILPARINKA

Darling

Murray

PORT LINCOLN

ADELAIDE

SYDNEY

ALBANY

ENCOUNTER BAY

MELBOURNE

TASMANIA

◄ In 1840, Edward Eyre was asked to explore a route from Adelaide to the west coast of Australia. He followed the coast round the Great Australian Bight. Tall cliffs and desert made the journey almost impossible. Today, there is a highway following much the same route and bearing his name.

THE POLES

Robert Peary, an American explorer, was the first man to reach the North Pole in 1909. He led six Arctic expeditions between 1891 and 1909 and proved that Greenland was an island. He used the local Inuit people and their methods to help him survive in the intense cold. ➤

Dog sledges are the traditional way of travelling over ice in the Arctic. They were used in Antarctica with great success but have gradually been replaced by other vehicles. ▼

◄ Memorial, in London, to Captain Scott who died in a blizzard on the return trip from the South Pole in 1912.

The race to the South Pole between the Norwegian, Roald Amundsen, and the British explorer, Robert Falcon Scott, is almost a legend.
On 14 December 1911, Amundsen reached the South Pole with four companions and sledges pulled by dogs. Scott's journey began from a different place and he used ponies instead of dogs. This led to disaster. He reached the Pole a month after Amundsen—and he and his companions all died on their return journey.

INTO THE AIR

The Wright brothers made the first recorded flight in an airplane on 17 December 1903. Today, planes and helicopters are used to provide a swift link with the outside world, and to map and explore areas that would otherwise be inaccessible.

The extent of the Amazonian rainforest and how it is being changed can only be assessed accurately from the air. Satellites give an overall picture, but the fastest way to reach any particular place, or make any detailed survey, is by plane. ▼

▲ Polar regions were explored from the air with great success. The first flight across the North Pole was made in a balloon by Amundsen and Nobile in 1926, and across Antarctica in 1929 by Byrd. Antarctic expeditions in the 1930s began using both traditional transport and spotter planes to survey their route.

UNDER THE SEA

◄ In 1960, Piccard and Walsh in the bathyscape, USS *Trieste*, reached a depth of 10,924 metres while investigating the Marianas Trench in the western Pacific.

In July 1969, Jacques Piccard drifted underwater along the length of the Gulf Stream, in a specially built six-man research submarine called *Ben Franklin*. As well as collecting valuable scientific information, the 30-day trip helped NASA investigate the effect on people of living for long periods in very cramped conditions—useful information for the space programme.

Between 1972 and 1975 manned submersibles explored the underwater ridge in the middle of the Atlantic Ocean where ocean bed is being formed, pushing Africa and South America apart at a rate of about 5 cm a year.

An unmanned submersible used to survey the continental shelf. It carries cameras and closed circuit television. ►

OUT INTO SPACE

In 1957, the USSR launched the first satellite, Sputnik 1, to orbit the Earth. By 12 April 1961, the first man in space, Yuri Gagarin, had orbited the Earth in Vostok 1. Four years later, Soviet astronaut Alexei Leonov made the first walk in space. He was out of the spacecraft for just 10 minutes. In 1984, American Bruce McCandless moved around freely in space using a powered back-pack.

Bruce McCandless—the first person to travel in space with no safety line attaching him to his spacecraft.▼

▲ Yuri Gagarin—the first person to orbit the Earth—his monument in Moscow.

Less than 12 years after Sputnik, on 21 July 1969, the American astronauts Neil Armstrong and Edwin Aldrin stepped out onto the surface of the moon. Having taken soil and rock samples and set up experiments, they returned to Earth. Later missions took moon buggies onto the surface and explored much further afield. The last manned lunar landing was launched on 5 December 1972.

Apart from Pluto, every planet in the solar system has been visited by a space probe. Space probes are robotic spacecraft, they can travel long distances transmitting back pictures and scientific information. At the present time, people can't make such journeys because they last many years and people need food, fuel and air for a return trip.

In August 1989, the space probe *Voyager 2,* flew past Neptune and discovered its dark spot—a vast storm in the atmosphere, similar to the red spot on Jupiter. Here scientists are studying pictures of Neptune transmitted by *Voyager.*▼

FACTS ABOUT EXPLORERS

Roald Amundsen
(1872-1928)
Norwegian explorer who was the first to navigate the north-west passage round North America 1903-6, and first to reach the South Pole in 1911.

James Cook
(1728-1779)
A great explorer who established that New Zealand was two islands in 1770, discovered South Australia in the same year, and rid his crews of scurvy. On his second great journey he crossed the Antarctic circle and discovered many new Pacific Islands. On his third, and final, journey he discovered the Hawaiian Islands before turning north to attempt the north-west passage.

Richard Burton
(1821-1890)
Larger-than-life character who wrote 43 books and hundreds of articles about his exploration all over Africa. Knighted in 1886.

Leif Ericsson
(c. AD 1000)
Probably one of the first Europeans to set foot in America. Discovered Vinland in AD 1000 which is now thought to have been around Cape Cod and Nova Scotia.

Christopher Columbus
(1451-1506)
Italian navigator who sailed on behalf of Spain. Travelled west to discover the East, reached America but never realised he had found a new continent.

Vasco da Gama
(1460-1524)
Portuguese navigator whose voyages from Portugal to India around Cape Horn in 1497-9 led to a whole new wave of exploration - and established Portugal as a major power.

Marco Polo
(1254-1324)
Italian traveller who spent many years in China.
His book about his travels inspired hundreds of explorers in later years.
He made others realise that there were rich and powerful civilisations outside Europe.

David Livingstone
(1813-1873)
Scottish missionary who travelled in Africa.
Discovered the Victoria Falls on the Zambezi River while crossing southern Africa from one side to the other.

Henry Morton Stanley
(1841-1904)
Sent by the *New York Herald* to find David Livingstone in Africa in 1869, Stanley was inspired to become an African explorer himself.
He travelled right across central Africa twice, once in each direction.
Ruthless and determined, Stanley plotted the course of many rivers and filled in the map of Africa for those who followed.

Ferdinand Magellan
(1480-1521)
Organised the first voyage around the world. Sailed round the southern tip of South America and named the Pacific Ocean.
Sadly, died before the circum-navigation was completed.

Robert Peary
(1856-1920)
American who first reached the North Pole in 1909.

Amerigo Vespucci
(1451-1512)
Italian merchant who on his second voyage to the "New World" in 1501, realised it was a whole new continent.
In 1507, Martin Waldseemuller, a cartographer, published the first maps of the "New World" and named the new land "America" in tribute to Vespucci.

INDEX